To Wendy,

WAKE UP *Girlfriend*

A collection of Girlfriend Stories to Grow on!

GOD BLESS

Missy Nyose

Wake Up Girlfriend: A collection of Girlfriend Stories to Grow on!. Copyright© 2019 by Angie CJ Sims

All rights reserved. This book is protected under the copyright laws of the United States of America. No part of this publication may be reproduced, stored in a retrieval system, or transmitted in any form or by any means, electronic, mechanical, photocopying, recording, or otherwise, without the prior written permission of the publisher.

Scripture quotations are from The King James Version of the Bible.

Cover Design: Marina Chetverikov.

For information and inquires, address Angie CJ Sims, Acworth, GA 30101

ISBN-13: 978-0-9972283-4-2

ISBN-10: 0-9972283-4-2

TABLE OF CONTENTS

Introduction

Why this book? Why now?
Why am I reading this?..14
How should I use it?..15

Chapter 1: Angie CJ Sims
Finding NEW Old Friends...................................18

Chapter 2: Cynthia Calhoun
Extending Grace..30

Chapter 3: Tanisha R. Lofton:
The Girlfriend I Needed…………………………..47

Chapter 4: LaSha' Marie
The Secret That Gave Me Wings……………..59

Chapter 5: Michelynn Moss
Girlfriends Don't Know Best............................78

Chapter 6: Connie Peltier
Blossie, My First Best Girlfriend.....................92

Chapter 7: April Y. Cunningham
Two Questions and a Statement....................103

Chapter 8: Yvonne Smith
Growth in Friendship……............................124

Conclusion……………………………….138

Thank you……………………………….141

About the Creator…………………….....144

Introduction

In August of 2018 I pondered on the idea of a book collaboration with Girlfriends. I had not written a collaboration book or even be apart of one. My thinking was that there were lots of women saying "I'm going to write a book one day," "I have a book in me," "God told me to write a book," "Everyone keeps telling me I should write a book," or the ever so popular "I wrote a book I just didn't put it down on paper yet!" I COULD NOT count how many times I have heard this from women that I've met.

I know lots of women who make their living creating authors through their publishing companies or book collaboration efforts. I figured that I'd just as well leave them to it and stay in "my lane." So I kept at the business of coaching women into their purpose, creating opportunities for women to collaborate in life and business and create new experiences with Girlfriends through the League of Girlfriends organization that was growing by leaps and bound.

Then like always God got all up in my business! I had resigned myself that I was busy enough and I wasn't going to embark on a Girlfriend's book collaboration. Then one day I was looking through files on one of my mother's memory sticks. I do this occasionally to see if I missed something my brothers and I could use or if I just see something new that could provide insight into her life. We loss my mother on Easter Sunday in 2015 after she suffered a stroke on December 16, 2014. My family had just moved to Acworth , Georgia from Northern New Jersey just 2 short months before my mother's sudden illness. Her mother and my dear, dear Nana, also departed us on February 20, 2015 just a few months before her passing. I never expected for my mother at 63 to leave us and although my Nana was 92 I didn't think that we would loose her either.

BUT if you would have told me that my mother would get sick and not be able to see her mother and her mother not be able to see her; then I would have seen how they just could not do without the other. It still would have hurt, but I could have seen it. I share this so that you can picture my state of mind as I looked through my mother's files with yet another-fresher eye.

Although I had put the idea of book collaboration out of my head, so I thought, it was never out of my heart. I wake up daily with the intention to do SOMETHING that can change a woman's life. Many times I call email or text a Girlfriend or just post something motivational or helpful on social media. Anything that can help a Girlfriend. So imagine my surprise as I looked through those files and found a Microsoft Word file named Girlfriend's Book Cover. Low and behold when I opened the file it was a draft of a book cover for a Girlfriend's collaboration book that I'd done a year or so ago. So then I did what I tend to do, gave into God! I threw up my hands and said, out loud, "OK God here you go again, I relent!"

So I put a post on Facebook that I am indeed creating this Girlfriends book collaboration and I have been so very, very blessed in this process and with the Girlfriends that signed on this journey with me.

Every gift is not meant to make you a millionaire however if you know you are truly listened to God in executing what you do and if you touch the lives of someone then you are truly rich.

"Surround yourself with only people who are going to lift you higher." – Oprah Winfrey

Why this book? Why now?

I'd pondered for months as to whether I should venture into creating a collaboration book. I mean, "Why should I?" Plenty of my friends and associates were creating collaboration books left and right and that was, "their lane." I'd just as well leave them to it. As a matter of fact, Taurea Vision Avant, who taught me how to write a book in less than 30 days, which I did, was a master at this. She has an entire online program dedicated to teaching business owners how to create an additional stream of income for your business by writing a book. She has also multiplied herself by empowering others to create book collaboration projects. So again, Why would I even consider doing a book collaboration when it simply was not "my lane."

You ever heard the saying, "If you wanna make God laugh, then make a plan?" Well I did just that. I'd planned to NOT create a book collaboration because

I was simply too busy. Then in just one day God changed my mind. The full story of how that happened if outlined in my introduction. Suffice to say I am so proud of what this collaboration has done for the seven women involved. It has been a transformational life experience that we each feel blessed to have been a part of.

WHY AM I READING THIS?

This book is for those who have experienced all different types of relationships ups and downs. Each girlfriend shares her story and her heart by exposing you to her experiences that have been, in most cases, life altering. Whether it is from betrayal or loyalty, each Girlfriend story will make a place in your heart that you can identify with. You may not have had the say exact experience but you will feel sincere and raw honestly in these stories. I often say that it's that, "It's not just me!" feeling that can save someone's life. These seven brave women have trusted me with the process and for that I am blessed. Read their stories and know what true freedom feels like in being able to share you without fear of retribution or reprisal.

How should I use it?

This book should not be considered a bible, for there is only one of those. I would, however, love for you to reference this book when considering your own situation. Take what is being shared in each girlfriend's experience as just that their experience. Whether you can identify with it or not you have the opportunity to see what someone else's life was like. Sometimes that's all it takes. Seeing what other relationships are made of or are void of may help you to appreciate or cast out what you have.

I believe that sharing each other without judgement is a way to find solace in our own lives and is truly a gift to anyone that we come in contact with. I applaud these girlfriends for laying it on the line. I believe that every woman needs a good girlfriend. Better yet every woman deserves a good girlfriend.

Read along you just might find one here.

Wake Up Girlfriend

Chapter 1.

Angela Sims

Finding New Old Friends

To by husband Dion Sims &
my Father Tony Anderson

If God never gave me 1 Girlfriend
you'd be more than enough!

Thank you for your wisdom, support
and for always cheering me on!

If you have heard me speak you may have heard my evolution to the mindset of having New Old Friends.

I've always had great Girlfriends. My very first Girlfriend who is still my very best Friend, Trish Parker, and I connected when we were just 7 years old. She was wearing a beautiful Easter Sunday dress on a regular Sunday. *No Shade* I was walking up the street to my Nana's house with jeans and a t-shirt on. I guess I missed service this day. I stuck my tongue out at her and she gave me the finger. Go figure friends for life. In addition to Trish my lifelong friends Tiffany Butts, Tawnya Russell, Ruth Coleman, Machelle Thomas, Donnet Swaby, Phyllis Toote and Jamila Perry were steadfast and the best friends a Girlfriend can have. Sure there have been other people who I'd become familiar with. I also had some amazing guy friends as besties that had my back throughout the years like John Mitchell, Shawn Alsop, Demetrius Carrol and Darius Pemberton. The two friends that I had the longest were my dad who is my ultimate champion, mentor and friend and my love and homeboy #1 my husband Dion. Dion and I played together as babies then dated in college, lost touch then stayed friends for 20 years and got married in 2006. No one has ever made me laugh as much or as often as Dion!

With so many close friends I was "good." One of my favorite sayings was, "You can't get no NEW Old Friends." I mean I lived by this saying. For years "The Mayor – pronounced May-A," which is my nickname for my husband because he knows and REMEMBERS everyone, would say to me that so in so said hi, they said they went to Reizenstein Middle School with you. My response would be "I don't know them and I don't remember them!" Awful right? He would try to describe them and it hardly ever sparked my memory of them. I left Pittsburgh when I was 18 to go to college and really, except for three months in 1993, never came back. Emotionally and mentally I was GONE from Pittsburgh before I even hit Penn State's campus. I came home for holidays but never really socialized with anyone except MY FRIENDS Trish, Tiff, Machelle, Ruth and Tawnya. Then when I moved to Jersey after college I hung out with who I was dating or Jamila, Donnet and Laura. Donnet and I worked together and were best friends so that was super great! So you see I didn't need any NEW friends, especially since you can't find any New Old Friends!

This may seem really strange but it's true. As a matter of fact when I was getting married to Dion and I made the announcement at work they didn't even know that I was dating seriously. It was NONE of their business because it was personal. Now come on Angie, I was taking myself wayyy to seriously.

Fast forward to 2014. My husband decided to switch careers and announced that we were moving to either

Texas or Atlanta! I picked Atlanta because I never liked the Texas heat or the length you have to drive to see another human being or grocery store. He arrived in Atlanta in September one month before me and Smooch (Christian) our 5 year old son.

He found us a beautiful home and spent time researching the area as I researched the schools and shopping nearby. He kept telling me how "nice" the people were. I say, "Yeah OK we'll see." Where was the positive attitude that my mother taught us? Anyway, when we arrived I spent time unpacking and sightseeing. Every day I discovered something new a museum, new eatery and all types of fantastic things. Then, since I'd been laid off from work back in July, I had to figure out what I would do for a living. The best part, if there's a good part, about being laid off , especially if you're an executive or have tenor is the severance package. I had over 14 years with the firm so I had some time to "figure it out." Also my husband told me that now was a good time to do 'Whatever I wanted' he encouraged me to start a coaching business, run my wedding and event planning business full time. "Whatever would make me happy," he said. What a blessing just hearing that was awesome. It makes ALL the difference when your spouse supports you the way that Dion always has.

So I looked through the numerous monthly magazines that are distributed to every town and county and I found a bunch of networking meetings and began to circle them with the intent on attending. Now remember the only people I knew of in the area was Dion and Smooch! I found an organization called Acworth Business Association. They were having a networking meeting just a few miles from my home. I went to the event which took place in a back room of a bar/restaurant. There were about 9 other people there some dressed in suits some business casual. They were all very nice and encouraged me to introduce myself, my business and what type of referral that I needed. I have been speaking publicly for over 20 years so I was totally up for this. They told me I had one minute. I was like, "Huh?, one minute," "But I just got to Georgia and I'm not sure which business I want to tell you about!" So here it goes..

"Hi my name is Angela Sims and I just moved here from Northern New Jersey a few weeks ago where I've been a full service wedding and event planner as well as florist and my ideal client is someone who is having an event or knows someone who is getting married." – whoa deep breath, ok I got through it. Everyone smiled and said thanks for coming.

After everyone did their introductions the meeting organizer mentioned when the next meeting was and how you could sign up to attend. I was ready to leave, remember this is business right? Then this lady came up to me and said, "Well Welcome to Georgia! I love your business and I want you to come to my event on Tuesday and I'll pay your way." I said – In my head – "Pay MY WAY?" "Where do they GROW these people at!" Well I was excited and did in fact attend her event which happened to be at the exclusive 5 star Marietta Country Club! The food was incredible ALL of the women were so nice and didn't mind sharing their business, clients and information to help me along. We were indeed not in Jersey/New York City anymore TOTO where the sentiment is "If you come near my clients, you die!" Atlanta and down south I venture to say is different.

This lady that I mentioned is Susan Guthrie. One of Cobb County's finest and a true connector of women and people everywhere. Susan and I are still friends today and she continues to do whatever she can wherever she can for people all over. Because of

Susan I met Diana Perez another great connector of women and true New Old Friend and then I met Taurea Avant through Diana. It is because of Taurea that I learned how to write my 1st book in less than 30 days and why I am now doing this collaboration. Each of these ladies are New Old Friends who I have grown with and together. They have been so significant in my journey and friendships that I know will last until the end of time.

Thank you God for my New Old Friends!!

"I love my husband, but it is nothing like a conversation with a woman that understands you. I grow so much from those conversations." –
Beyoncé

Special Thank you to my pre-sale supporters

Cea Alford

Geri Looker

Geron Anderson

Kym Hampton

Nathan & Leslie Anderson

Wanda Pearson

Tawnya Peek-Russell

Mark Willis

Zalima Alexander

Judi Smith-Olgetree

Shawn & Tamika Alsop

Robert & Laura Montgomery

Sheila Tibbits

Melissa Brown-Haynes

Dr. Jerrica Dodd

Micki Jackson

Ronnell Anderson

Karla Bernard

Wake Up Girlfriend

Chapter 2.

Cynthia Calhoun

Extending Grace

To my late grandmother, my amazing mom, my wonderful kids and the greatest grand babies "ever"... I love you more than the stars in the sky! Jason...words don't express how much I love you! I appreciate your amazing and everlasting support! You all make me who I am!

Oh no, she didn't! I thought she was a friend! A real woman wouldn't…! I tell you what, hell will freeze over before I let her into my life again!

We've all been there. We've all said something similar…maybe even worse! Yes, we've judged someone who offended us, hurt our feelings, or made us "mad". Here's one such story.

※

Grace and I met at a Girl's Day Spa Party. We hit it off, enjoyed good conversation, and exchanged business cards. We reconnected several months later and became fast friends! We had regular Friday night dinners and did a lot together. We quickly formed a strong sisterhood, had common goals, likes and dislikes, laughed a lot at the same things, and talked on the phone for hours at a time! We exercised together, did 5k races, watched sports, went to "single girl" workshops, and planned parties.

It was a great friendship! One night we were hanging out at my house, when her guy called. After just a couple minutes her tone changed, and she asked if she could have some privacy. Of course I said yes, as she went into the bathroom and closed the door. I purposely turned the TV up. Then after about 90 minutes, I got this uneasiness in my gut. 3 hours later, I woke up and went to check on her. She was hysterical! This man broke up with her "on the phone!" We talked and cried together 'til around 3 a.m. Then I made her spend the night…and in "girl code fashion", I attached myself to her hip. I checked on her daily. We cried together. We were mad together! I was her sounding board! When he called to come pick up "his things", she asked me to be there when he came. Of course! I had to be there to barely speak when he walked in, to shake my head, and give him the up/down… side-eye! You know the drill!

Then... I met Jason. Months had gone by since "that other dude," and Grace and I had been a pair. I kept her occupied so she wouldn't obsess. Jason and I were now always together, so she became a little weird! But it was literal magic between Jason and I! God literally "spoke to me" audibly, that I was going to fall in love...and boy did I ever! Love at first sight! I believed...I just never thought it could happen to me! That story in another book. So, we were instantly inseparable...together...ALL THE TIME!

Before I realized, weeks had passed and Grace and I hadn't had more than a quick conversation or dinner here and there. I was busy cultivating this surprising new relationship that God had sent into my life. I was not looking for love...and yet it had hit me straight over the head!!!

Grace kept saying, "Hey, don't give him all your time! You know men come and go, but sisters are forever! Girlfriends are always there for each other!" She was still hurting and jaded, so I let things slide. She had verbally expressed how desperately she wanted to get married, yet here I was…madly in love with the guy of "our" dreams and love had swooped me up in two months. Jason and I met in March and he proposed in May! It was all the right things for me at all the wrong time for her! She became distant, and the distance grew wider between us, as Jason and I became closer. As much as I hated the fact that Grace was hurting, I couldn't stop cultivating this new relationship! I "knew" where I was supposed to be…and it was at Jason's rib for the rest of our lives!

Just 57 days into this new relationship, he popped the question. I'll never forget the sheer surprise, excitement, and joy of it all! I heard God's voice the night I met Jason say that I was going to fall in love! God didn't even say "we", He just spoke it to me. God knew I needed to be sure of two things:

1. That I "knew" His voice.

2. That I needed to fully trust and rely on Him.

In April, Jason got a job offer in Topeka, KS! He called and asked if I thought he should take it and I reluctantly said yes. I thought to myself, "I don't do long distance relationships." So I wondered what this meant for our future! The company would only transport one car so he asked if I would drive down with him that Friday, after the movers came. He would fly me back that Sunday evening. He asked if I was coming over that night, but I knew he'd be busy preparing for the movers, and I didn't wanna be in the way. He wanted me there so I came over that night and …he proposed! Every time I turned over in my sleep, I would run my fingers across the ring on my left hand in shock; and I'd feel intense joy! Just as strongly, I then felt a pang in my stomach. "OMG! How will I tell Grace?!" I had a dream that night about breaking the news to her. All this love and joy, and I'm concerned about telling her. So when I finally did tell her, the response was exactly as I saw it in my dream! "It's too soon," she said abruptly. Just burst my little love bubble and then she went "ghost" for several weeks. When she resurfaced, she said she'd just been really busy at work, but explained that she truly was happy for me, just shocked that it happened so quickly. She wanted us to have dinner so she could "see the ring!" As hard as she tried, her reaction was less than enthusiastic, and her response and comments were from my dream…verbatim!

Then in October, Grace met Gavin! I was so-o-o happy for her! They looked good together and she glowed! We were back to our happy place! Gavin was charming and humorous…but also quite flirtatious. Grace was very jealous and argumentative, so when he flirted with our waitress or the girl at the bowling shoe rental, or "wherever"…it was tense! They were Oil and Water! We "double dated" a lot…but the nights always ended in fighting! Jason and I usually spent the next day "talking" them thru their drama! It was exhausting! I finally said, "Listen, I believe Gavin loves you, but I just don't see the compatibility!" Her response was, "Well I want to get married, and I want a baby! He keeps asking me what I want for Christmas, and I told him, if you don't buy me an engagement ring, I don't want anything!" Wait, what?! I just didn't understand how she couldn't see what was so obvious to us. We were on the phone one night talking about yet, another episode of the "Grace and Gavin Show"! I said, "You know I love you and I want to see you happy, but are you…really happy? You guys fight "All. The. Time!" Do you want *this* for the rest of your life?! If you're always mad now when you go out, what do you think marriage will be like?! You'll either stay at home or go out and be mad! Remember this is your second marriage, if this doesn't work, a lot of men may see you as damaged goods!" Her response…"Well, I'm 34! I want a baby before 40, and I want to get married!" My response was "So, do you want to "get" married Grace, or do you want to "be" married?! There is a difference. Don't get caught up in the ring, the wedding, and the idea." There was silence. Then…she yells, "Why can't you just be happy for me?! You're in love. You've got your man! You're planning your wedding! OMG! Just be happy!" and with that, she hung up!

It was the middle of December and I didn't talk to her again until she called me Christmas Eve. She called and screamed into the phone that they were engaged, and the wedding is February! Then she stops and says, "Oh, wait, when is your wedding again?!" I slowly replied…really, Grace?!" Our wedding has been planned since May. It's April 3rd.

Remember?" "Oh, I forgot," she said. "I guess since yours was planned first, I should at least plan mine after yours." I said…"Yes Grace, you should! I've gotta go."

A chain of events lead up to the rest of this story…but in summary, Jason and I got married April 3rd and Gavin and Grace got married in May. They were married for a few months when the drama kicked in! They called constantly asking for help. She ended up on anxiety meds, and eventually he left! We had moved to Kansas by now, and didn't know all the details, but what we did know was not good! I also knew that "once again" she wasn't responsive to my emails and calls; but Jason and I were newlyweds! We didn't have the time nor the desire to notice much of anything, other than each other! We had bought our "first" home, and picked out new furniture, together! We were busy…being newlyweds! One day we were preparing to go buy artwork, and I heard Jason's phone ring. I could hear his end of the conversation and soon realized he was talking to Grace, and I could hear her yelling in his ear! I thought something was wrong! Then I heard her basically fussing him up one side and down the other!

As I walked into the office...she hung up in his face! He was sitting there literally staring at the phone in shock! But...He never lost his cool. He never raised his voice. He never became defensive. Basically, Gavin and Grace had separated, and she was having a meltdown in Jason's ear. He said, "It's okay! She's just stressing and she needs someone to blame." I fell in love with him all over again...and I haven't heard from Grace since that day.

I've searched on Facebook, by her maiden name, but nothing. Gavin has reconnected with Jason and they may talk once a year; but I've lost all contact with Grace. I considered her a dear friend, and it sucked to lose that; but it was not until I began putting this story together, that I began to heal! Emotions came out as I wrote. Rather than clap-back with the "Oh no, she didn't! A real woman wouldn't" speech, I acknowledge that deep pain can extend us beyond reason. That was 13 years ago and I'm just now getting free of feelings that I didn't even know I had. This marriage extended Grace far beyond who she was. She "was" A Real Woman. She "was" a real friend. She was just "extended"! I'm grateful that God heals! I now have the ability to be extended past hurt to healing and past pain to purpose. I'm grateful that God heals and I pray that she has found healing also. He has extended His grace towards me. So I, a "Real Woman," who is now healed, am "extending grace" to another "Real Woman."

Special Thank you to my pre-sale supporters

Lloyd Leftridge

Camille Porter

Jerlyn Owens

Amaryllias Dixon

Lawayna Gillette

Barbara Harrison

Alice Johnson

Terri Crook

Asia Kuykendall

Janice Jones-Holley

Kemberlee Musa

Michelle Blackwell

Keva Deas

Stephanie Rolle

Linda Pelham

Lillian Chapman

Robin Clark

Keyetta Williams

Dieko Toyin Adelaja

Liz Williams

Angela Bolden

Lucy Dawson

Kyle Dawson

Andrea Loyd

Tiquita Stewart

Miriam Williams

Delijah Williams

Sherry Hunt

JoAnna Wright

Rhonda Barnes

Tonya Harris

Lenora Ranson Anderson

Roslyn Robertson

Dr. JeNeen Ridgeway

Gregory Cousin

Lavetta Bernard

Selena Parker

Tammy Galloway

Pastor Debra Hill

Ebony Mason

Brenda Willis

Windy Green

Temi Tope

Mitchell Pugh

Wake Up Girlfriend

Larry Darnell Haqq

Opal Harris

Minister Rochelle Cross

Lossie Savage

Sandra Jones

Alice Bolden

Linda Roberson

Earlene Anderson

Dr. Carol Bolden

Holly Hamman

Sherry Calhoun

Georgia Hill

Zulekia Atkinson

Rhonda Jones

Chapter 3.

Tanisha R. Lofton

The Girlfriend I Needed

To my Dad, David Richard Thomas. May you rest in peace and know everything I do is with you in mind. I love you Daddy.

For as long as I could remember, I've always gotten along better with boys than I have with girls. And it seemed fitting since I was what you'd call a tomboy. Sure, I had my girly moments where I played with my Barbie dolls, and kitchen sets and played house, but I also had my Tonka trucks, little green Army men, superhero action figures and went looking for bugs in the woods and creeks. I like to think I had balance, or the best of both worlds, in my amazing childhood. As an adult, I still get along better with men than I do women and I've never thought about why that is and just accepted it was to be so.

When I think of my girlfriends throughout my life, I always come back to one person, her name is Daisel Brown. Daisel, or Dayz (pronounced Daisy) for short, is one of my oldest, dearest and truest friends from back home in Erie, Pennsylvania. We met when I was 16 years old in the summer of 1991 and were inseparable until I moved away to Mississippi in 1995 but even then our friendship has remained strong and distance hasn't diminished it. May have something to do with the fact that five years later she moved to Mississippi as well, but I think our bond is deeper than that. In fact, I know it is! To this very day, the bond we share is as intact as it was in 1991 and I often wonder what I did to deserve a friend as good as her. She is my confidante, my voice of reason, my ear when I need one to bend and my cheerleader when I've stepped out of my comfort zone to explore a new desire and goal.

As good as she has been and still is to me, makes me ask myself the question, "Have I been the same to her?" I strive to be the kind of friend that I need but I feel as if I fall short in the delivery category. The older I get the more I realize that I am somewhat of a complex woman and it really takes a special person to get close enough to know me and patient enough to stick around once you do. I won't call her a saint but God sure did give her the patience of one when it comes to me. I pray to Him often and seek wisdom and guidance on a plethora of things including how to be the type of girlfriend that I need in my life. I possess the characteristics and qualities needed to be a great friend, or so I think, based on what I look for in a friend. But I find myself longing for that group of girlfriends here in Georgia that I can hang out with, share with, do fun activities with and even cry with. Don't get me wrong, I know some great ladies that I have lots of fun with, like Kristina Hamilton who was one of my first girlfriends when I moved to Georgia, Ieshea Lattimore who I met because of our military service in the Air Force; Donna Etheridge who I met through Kristina and inspires me each day and she probably doesn't even know it; and a few others but there is always something missing. I feel like the odd woman out more often than not and I think back to growing up and hanging in the backyard of my Grandmother's house playing football and other sports with the neighborhood boys. Did it set the precedent for my future friendships where I would find it easier to talk to and get along naturally with the guys versus the girls?

I am a mother of boys, four of them, and I often tease and say God knew what he was doing when he gave me sons and no daughters because I'm just not equipped to deal with girls and girl stuff. The emotions, tears and drama that are associated with girls, emotions that I often times fight within myself, make me uncomfortable and I don't know how to quite deal with them. I don't like crying and will fight tears at all costs no matter how many times I am told that crying is normal and cleansing. I've had other women tell me before that I'm not sensitive enough or I am different from most women because I view things like a man would. Maybe hanging with my uncle's and some of their friends then having sons gave me a different perspective and outlook to things. If women are from Venus and men are from Mars then I guess I lie somewhere in between the two. And I'm not alone in my world of testosterone because Dayz is also a mom of four sons but with her I allow myself to be vulnerable enough to have the girly feelings accompanied with the occasional tears.

I can remember some of the early memories of our friendship where we'd dress alike, liked the same music and went everywhere together. We were dating cousins at the time, which is how we met and grew close, and it was as if I found a kindred spirit who understood all my emotions and ways even when I didn't understand them. There isn't anything I didn't tell her because I knew that it would always stay between us and that she'd help me figure out what needed figuring. We'd talk for hours about everything imaginable and I didn't have to pretend to be ok if I wasn't and she never had to pretend with me. Even now, as grown women with families to take care of I can pick up the phone at any time and talk her ear off and we laugh and cry and promise to take time and vacation. Then we get back to life and vacation must wait.

When I was diagnosed with fibromyalgia in 2012, I didn't know how to get through my days. My way of life and everything I was used to had to change to accommodate low energy and high pain levels. I was now living in Georgia and she was still in Mississippi and I felt like I had no one to talk to about the differences in my body that were out of my control. Dayz helped me research and come to understand what I was going through and ways that I could help myself deal with the pain and changes. I was no longer able to be as active and do the physical things that I'd taken for granted and had always done with ease which caused a deep depression within me. Depression and anxiety seemed to be the two terms to best describe me for many years after my diagnosis and recently my life changed in the worst way I could imagine: I found myself faced with many losses in a short period of time. In a matter of five months I lost my father, I lost my job, I lost my home, I lost some people that I thought were my friends, I lost my faith and I lost my will to live. What I didn't lose was Dayz and she wasn't even physically here. While she tackled the tangible losses that could be helped using local resources, yes she looked up what resources were available to me in Georgia from her home and office in Mississippi, and helped me see that although things looked bleak right now I still had so much to live for, my girlfriend and Sister in Christ, Tawanna Bryant-Osborne got to work on my faith! These two ladies pulled me back from the brink and I am eternally grateful to them.

Several years after my own health changes, Dayz called me to tell me of her own health issues and I cried because I was afraid and didn't want to lose her. She waited to tell me because she knew how I would receive the news and even with her going through what she was, she put my feelings first. WOW! I wanted to go visit but she wasn't up for visitors and I didn't fight to make the trip to see her. Should I have? Should I have ignored her request to heal and get better first and went to be by her side anyway? I wanted to be the rock for her that she has always been for me but I wasn't even strong enough to handle her news without breaking down and I felt so guilty about it then; I still do. I want a girlfriend that is there for me even when I think I don't need her to be but may want her to be and I wasn't that girlfriend to her. Do I know how to be that girlfriend, the one that I need? Can I let past hurts, bad decisions and wrong moves go so that I can move forward and be the girlfriend I need to someone else? I see glimpses of her in me every now and then and the glimpse fades. As I work on finding me I think I will find that Girlfriend and I can't wait to be introduced to her. The great thing is I have time and opportunity to be the great friend I desire by following her example.

Special Thank you to my pre-sale supporters

Coreen Harvey

Mike Carter

Myra King

Minister Naheede T. Brooks

Linda D. Roberts

Jade Dawson

Wake Up Girlfriend

Aleea Blocker

A. Anne Prince

Marsha L. Thomas

James & Michelle Thomas

Stephen & Courtney Thomas

Denise Thomas

RaVaire & Rechelle Prince

Howard & Annjerrica Hollis

Cliff & Falecia Bibbs

Donna Howard

Tracy Segura, Sr.

Gwendolyn Rose Mbuvi

Andrew Nixson & Terinique Keys

Darmita Cox

Vernon Hartley

Chapter 4.

LaSha' Marie

"The Secret That Gave Me Wings"

Dedicated to my children who inspired me:
Alexander and Sanea…
You're my light source that keeps me!

Often times we reminisce about the easy chapters of life. The slight moments when you feel free and unstressed without a care in the world. This may differ from person to person. Some may relish in their times of victories however, I hold my most treasured moments growing up in the inner city of Detroit, Michigan. The 80's was the era when neighbors were close. Where Mrs. Avery next door chastised you right in the presence of your mom and was the spy when your parents were away. Where well-manicured lawns were a mile wide in the middle of the ghetto and you could find gang affiliated tags painted on the sides of gas stations nearby. It was then that I began to be shaped into the woman that I am today. My values, traditions, friendships and goals were formed with women I still today hold dear to my heart. Girlfriends!! No matter if we are miles apart or months between phone calls; we still lean on each other for support, upliftment, encouragement, growth and accountability. Real friendships remain stable even during the storms. Like vines of a plant we are sisters, growing in one another and multiplying in clusters.

30 Years a Girlfriend!

It was around 1986 on Murray Hill Street. A west side community where sisterhood cultivated on concrete porches and "spend the night" occasions between growing girls with curious minds. I always said that I'm very lucky to have 30 year sisterships with not only one; but three women that became intricate parts of my life; Tia, Mieka and Vee. All of them, while different in every way are similar in that they want to conquer life with their own families. They are women with multiple degrees, stable careers all while being awesome active moms who are business savvy.

I often categorized this period of my childhood as "Being Released". I was the new girl on the block; new school, new area and new soon to be friends....Girlfriends. Trying to fit in wasn't a need for this Murray Hill "crew". Both boys and girls huddled together at whoever's house allowed us to be exactly what we were; kids. We brought laughs, gossip or discussed the latest beef (conflict) between kids. Parents lent ears, a cup of sugar or even packages of meat during hard times. Those evenings when parents would speak at length, us girls would scatter in the house with hopes that the talks linger a little longer. It became habit to jump on a high bed, cross our legs and whisper secrets yet to be shared. No use for phones when your best friends are across the street or fourteen houses over on the next block. For me, this was a time to escape and enjoy being a child. I was new to the area for reasons I would blame myself for years later. In my old neighborhood I was accustomed to friendships, play Aunts and being surrounded by a mixed race. I was forced to give this up. Not because I had done something wrong, but because I gave life to words I had never said out loud before. Once they hit the ears of other people I couldn't take them back. The meaning of the words and those acts would soon surface exposing wounds and a state of total confusion.

It never had to be a particular day for "Girl Talk". These moments of loud cackling and sometimes annoying laughter was between long walks to and from school. But from 5th grade to high school graduation it was always the best time when you could spend the night anywhere but home. To this day I still remember weekends spending the night with my best friend, Tia. I always admired her home. Conservative and inspiring with textures and tones with art work adorned in lilac accents, which was her mother's favorite color. If I was lucky her mom (a beautician) would style my hair in the latest asymmetrical cut, French roll or pump waves. Tia and I would walk to the corner store and come home with bags filled with junk. We'd climb on the bed to catch up on the latest boy crush, school games, fashion and how our parents simply drove us crazy. I was just approaching eleven years old; by this time I knew Tia and her family very well. She was like a God-sister, I could tell her anything. So it was "releasing" to share my story especially since things in my own household had changed so drastically.

This weekend stay was no different than any other. Bags packed, clean pajamas while listening to melodies of music blaring in the background. So, while eating a bag of Red Hot Cheetos, I said, "I was molested by my step-father until the day he left," which Tia knew was 3 months prior. This is a man that raised me as my Dad, my protector since the age of two. Those words I think shocked her, almost frozen in time with no distinct expression on her face. She allowed me to talk and as always she listened. I explained this same secret I shared with a family in my old neighborhood.

"So you told someone?" she stated.

I replied, "Yes!" I went on to tell her that I told a family on the Eastside of Detroit prior to moving to my new block.

Parts of that day I often relive in my head. The mother that I shared my story with actually fainted. **I thought I killed this lady by sharing the secret I was told never to share.** I watched this woman hit the floor so hard I felt the floor shake under my 10-year-old feet. All three of us, in unison, crying as I released this burden and weight off my chest.

Still listening, Tia sat there like a shell as I spoke these unbelievable words. She would ask me questions like, "So what happened after?" and "What did your mom do?" She uttered in between questions with an, "Oh Wow!" I simply stated, "Nothing happened, nothing happened at all." Very little changes happened in my house even after the elementary school social worker was called. I don't think Tia wanted to pry, I think she just wanted to be a good friend and be there. As children will do, we went back to laughing, dancing, and eating high calorie snacks.

Most times, when you reveal a secret you allow others to judge you, question your truth, pick apart your story, and even signal other predators of their next victim. I went through my formative teenage years suppressing images, coping with the "act" and the damages that it causes to a whole family unit. From the time I gave life to those words, I don't believe I saw my Mother the same. Not because she wasn't loving or she didn't believe me but because she became lost within herself and the days went by one drink at a time. The reasons why he left didn't matter. HE WAS GONE! My mom had amazingly resilient strength. Caring for my brother and me as a single parent, with dynamic family support. But there were a lot of days in battle. My mother put her kids first even while being a substance abuser. While other kid's moms or dads were plagued with being victims of the crack epidemic she defied many other inner-city odds. When I was a child I used to think alcoholism was the lesser addiction. I would mature to understand that chemical abuse of any kind plays on the same field. One not superseding the other. Now picture being a child living everyday trying to survive under your own roof before you even open the door to hit the streets of Detroit.

On those days when my Mother couldn't deal with life, I stepped right in; either by taking a "jitney" to the store for groceries or filing out her renewal forms for our Section 8 home (all prior to age 16). This role reversal built my character and taught me that life happens and you just keep going. For all that people thought about my mom; family was first for her. Stylish, creative and very protective about who she had around her children. I like to think I became an extension of who she was and what I believe, who she aspired to be. All of my girlfriends were close to my mom even when they respectfully bumped heads with her. When she passed away at the age of 44 years old, each one of those girlfriends allowed me to take of their energy. Tia gave me boldness while Vee lent me her spiritual vision and well, Mieka taught me that success can be obtained with little people rooting for you.

We maintain these relationships today, celebrating births, degrees and/or marriages. I had two kids (10 years apart), two marriages, a career, God given talent that is multi-faceted. I'm simply a motivating spirit to uplift everyone despite trauma.

In 2015, I thought I had it all figured out. Though I had down moments, I was still winning in many areas of my life but the devil will test you. I added a daily walk to my routine therapy. One day I found myself lost, dazed and confused. My phone rang and it was Tia calling to do a "buddy check". We always had a way of checking on each other. So it was surprising to me when I saw Tia's car pulling up next to me in my complex. I immediately started crying because I had just been released after seven days from Lakeview Mental Hospital after an attempted suicide. This girlfriend drove over 1,300 miles to see about her sister. To make sure I was ok and to command me back on track. She brought hope and that fierce attitude with bold confidence. I was almost 41 years old and I still felt like I was that 11 year old seeking shelter in her friendship.

My message is my motto to all: Nothing stops you but YOU. Even if you fail 10 times, keep going another round. Never let anyone keep you in your past, it doesn't define you. It didn't matter that people questions who I am or what I obtained despite my Mom having all the stains in life; teen mom, welfare recipient and alcoholism. I take honor in knowing that although I had many hands that preyed upon me, years of depression, a suicide attempt; I still broke generational curses. Your purpose is affirmed by God not people. I've learned these valuable lessons:

1. Your truth is according to you. Speak it, share it!

2. We are women of soil. Know that you are able to produce and reproduce!

3. Healing is the prerequisite of everything standing before you.

4. Parents can love you and still make mistakes. I HAD THE BEST MOM EVER!!!!!

5. Be a healer of yourself FIRST. A woman living in damage can't arm anyone!

6. Find your inside-out-kinda happiness. Chose to live whole, self-sufficient and according to no one else's rules but yourself.

7. Be fearless in your aspirations. We are our biggest critic and enabler.

8. Allow no one to keep you in your past. Let them cast doubt in who you are because you're walking in HIS destiny according to HIS plan for YOU!

As sister's we must lend to each other the power of regeneration. Life isn't that planned out list or views of perfection. I'm a child God given in the vessel of Tony Francene Golson-Dawson. In spite of all the stains of life; NOTHING HAS STOPPED ME! And lastly, forgive yourself. I went on to have five predators. I felt like I had a "TOUCH ME" sign above my head. One violent unreported rape, domestic violence in the form of emotional and verbal abuse, morbid obesity, low self-esteem and promiscuity. I learned to walk in God's destiny in being true to who I was called to be.

"I want to dress up my insides so it will think it walked in the wrong door. I just wanted it to find another host, and shout boldly to it, "you no longer live here!" That's the Freedom of Depression.

Special Thank you to my pre-sale supporters

My Mentor: Jerry Lawrence of Detroit, MI (My Mentor in Human Capital Management & Lifecycle Recruitment)

James Anderson Auburn, Alabama

William Dejohn Colclough Atlanta, Georgia

Yorel Overstreet Maricopa, Arizona

Wake Up Girlfriend

Lynn Kirby (Mentor in Healthcare Sales and Recruiting Compliance) who lost her battle with cancer.

Marie D. (Snellville, Georgia)

Mr. Jennings of Mt. Elam Missionary Baptist Church Opelika, Alabama

Zawadi Tamu Detroit, Michigan

Ministers Mr. & Mrs. Thomas Allen Auburn, Alabama

Adrienne Jones Gwinnett, GA

My Girlfriends: Tamieka G., Tia W., Valerie P.; I simply adore you!

Todd Dixson Detroit, Michigan

Meshia Mitchell Macon, Georgia

Wake Up Girlfriend

I Am One

I don't sit alone in this cold lonely world
There are many touched just like me
We all face the same fate
Of recovery from self-hate
And shame that they dealt
Upon the little ones they felt

I Am One

Healing the wounds would hurt just as much
To forget the images of his touch
Locking the door would not keep me safe
But saying my prayers would keep me a saint

I Am One

The images won't leave and haunts me by eve
Will anyone help this little child please?
God has me near so I'll trust in his sight
To get me through another day's night
Cause I'm trapped in fear and the memories are still near

I Am One
The Step-daddies I fear
Even though I'm his sweet dear

So keep me safe and clear
So I won't be touched again down near

I Am One

There are plenty just like me

And silent they shall be

Sheltering the pain that was caused
From the innocence that was lost

I ...Am... One...

By: LaSha' Marie

Wake Up Girlfriend

Chapter 5.

Michelynn Moss

Girlfriends Don't Know Best!

To my loved ones whom supported me and have been a major part of my life; my husband Eric Moss Sr, sons Roberto, Matthew, Eric Jr, my parents Donald(RIP)and Deloris, brother DJ(RIP). I Love You.

My girlfriend experience begins with beautiful women of all ages, colors, and nationalities who grew up in dysfunctional poverty-stricken and middle and upper-middle-class homes. Some had two parents and some had one. Some had guidance and love some did not. We may not have known our parent's circumstances or struggles that shaped them into the people they became. This in turn shaped us into the "girlfriends" we would become. Unfortunately, they may have imposed their pain on us. Moreover, some of us imposed our issues on our children, spouses, and girlfriends. I began as a woman whose soul was in turmoil with many challenges but now I am a woman who overcame self-doubt and learned to lean on her inner strength and peace, and embraced loving herself.

I am writing this chapter to tell my "girlfriend" that I forgive her for the love, loyalty and respect that I bestowed upon her that she clearly took for granted and didn't know how to give it back. I know I am still a work in progress and GOD is still working on me. I also want to ask her to please accept my apology for the things I did to hurt her. It was never my intention.

I am not sorry for having to walk away from things and people who did not allow me to grow who did not truly know me. I am sorry that I allowed you to take me out of character of being Missy Moss. I changed into a person I could not even recognize. I allowed myself to let depression creep in and it was very difficult to come out of it, and it was hard to believe that my girlfriends would abandon me. I was devastated and didn't know how I was going to live without them.

While trying to start this project I experienced different emotions. This is something that I always wanted to do and I did not want to miss such an amazing opportunity. Write something to my girlfriends? A happy story or a sad story? I thought about the wonderful women in my life, especially the ones I fellowship with at Women's Bible Study on Wednesday mornings. I thought, this could not be that hard, but it brought up so many emotions. Thank God to those of you that still have that girlfriend from elementary school, the cheerleading squad, the girlfriend you met in new members class at church or at training class for that new powerhouse job that was going to take you to the next level. Don't forget the girlfriends that let you cry on their shoulder when that not so nice guy broke your heart. However, what do you do when you had more heartbreak from your girlfriends than your man?

In the same way that nothing prepares you to be a parent, no matter how much advice you receive, nothing prepares you on how to be a girlfriend. Isn't friendship about having morals and values, having manners and respect and having love and integrity?

Why do we have to turn to social media to find a girlfriend on the Meetup app? Why is it that we as women cannot get along? We need to break those generational curses.

It is so befitting that I am participating in a Bible study class, "Rachel and Leah: What two sisters teach us about combating comparison." This book is by Nicki Koziarz a story of dysfunction. Why do we as women compare ourselves to others and ask "Why not me. Why is her hair longer, butt bigger, clothes nicer, does her man love her more than mine loves me? Why was I not blessed to have that job, why is she wearing red bottoms and I am not." Was it favoritism that one child got over another or heartbreak from a wounded man that shaped us into these low self-esteem women that we have become? **We need each other any way you look at it!** We are still a village and it does not stop when our children become adults. We actually need a girlfriend more when you become an empty nester. I need a girlfriend to talk to and go to happy hour with. To let my hair down and vent about all that has gone on in my life this past week. I need a girlfriend to cry and laugh with. Nevertheless, I reluctantly had to do this girlfriend thing alone and it felt so unnatural.

I was in a bad space in this particular season and I felt like the world was closing in on me and I had some girlfriends, two in particular, that weren't there. They didn't even like each other and they came from two different sides of the tracks. One was ***boogie*** and one was ***hood***. One was corporate the other was a blue-collar worker, and they both thought they knew what was best for me. Neither took their own advice.

So, in comes the comparison. They had a little bit more education than me, maybe making more money so I trusted and praised them more than I should have. I treated them like they were Oprah or Iyanla Vanzant. It was like I didn't have my own mind at times. For years, I respected them and believed their so-called wisdom. My other girlfriends told me they were not my friends. I never thought they were more intelligent than I was. I just felt they were more knowledgeable in certain areas so I listened. At no time was I praying and asking God for answers *he unfortunately was nowhere in the picture.*

Back to that season in my life. I was still not leaning on GOD, just listening to my friends and very frustrated with life. I decided I was checking OUT! Therefore, because of bad choices I chose to make I ended up in a homeless shelter in Atlanta, GA. Yes! Shocker. I was scared and alone and trying to be strong. I was not eating, sleeping and I shared a room with Big Momma and two other women. I was sleeping with my money in my underwear because I did not know these people. I felt like I was in jail. I was stressed out as hell and back and forth to the doctor. I asked myself what the HELL have I done to myself and to my family. I have to make this right but, I don't know how. I'm not ready to go back to Memphis. I need some time to get my head together. I did not want to burden my kids, my mother is getting old and I did not want to burden her so no worries. I HAVE MY GIRLFRIENDS..... or do I? I wanted to go home to my comfort zone. Therefore, I stopped listening and following the leader. I told myself that I have to put my big girl panties on and go home and face my demons. So I did.

That is when all hell broke loose with my so-called girlfriends. They were furious with me. They were livid that I didn't DO WHAT THEY TOLD ME TO DO! So now, the **hood** meets **boogie** and they became allies. They said I was lying about my health, that I used it as an excuse to go home. What was I supposed to do, wander in the wilderness while they were in the comfort of their homes? I was blocked on their social media. They turned their backs on me and I was devastated! They started calling each other hanging out at different events and I was the topic of discussion. I was so hurt, so I finally decided to depend on GOD, which I regret not doing in the first place. He led me to a great therapist. *Yes, people go get some help if you need it.*

So always lean on GOD, it is not about education it is not about your age, your tax bracket the car you drive or the house you live in. It is about loyalty, trust, respect and communication. It's about keeping the girlfriend code, realizing that we are in this together. We all have our struggles, our issues, our strengths and weaknesses. We are all the same. We want Love, Peace, Acceptance, and Understanding!!

I have moved on. I still love these individuals and I have forgiven them and I wish them well. My Lord always orders my steps and I will never forget that. I let the old girlfriend in me go for a new and improved me. I took my experiences good and bad and refocused them on **the New girlfriend I have become**. I am so happy for this awakening, the good and the old. I am like the woman who had the issue of blood in the bible who came from behind pushing through the crowd reaching the front to receive her blessings. *I am ready to see all things new.*

"It is safer on the waves with Jesus than in the boat without him"-Dr. Adrian Rogers

"To all the women who carry the torch of courage, stroke the fires of confidence, and spread the light of spirit. You are an inspiration and I honor you."-Sue Patton Thoele

Wake Up Girlfriend

Special Thank you to my pre-sale supporters

Eric Shane Moss Sr.

Deloris Jones

Roberto and Sarah Cruz Jr

Eric Shane Moss Jr.

Matthew Khalani Cruz

Nsongi and Sandra Jones proprietors of The Ivy School 278 Willow Street Teaneck, NJ and i-Tech Trucking LLC

Teressa Wilkins

John Smith

Susan Parks

Paula Jones

Ja'Mara Taylor

Jana Welch

Bianca Chang

Tiffany Mcneal

Mary Kearney

Cynthia Kammen

Jalmari Smith proprietor of Psiberactive
Entertainment

Felicia Groves

R. Shaunny Tatum

Marcia Clark

Tara Moore

Gail Blundon

Nicole Wilkins

Vanessa Robinson

Shelly Pearson

Kenya Littrice

Jeanna Berry

Lillian Thomas

Edward A. Green LL

Daria Surratt

Marchell Riggins

Nina DeBose

Berlin Rouse Family

Donald R. Jones

Donald Smith

Arthur and Margaret Moss

Geraldine G. Avery

Pem Shaw

Vanessa Kendrick Robinson

Wake Up Girlfriend

Chapter 6.

Connie Peltier

Blossie, My First Best Girlfriend

To my husband Lawrence, my mom Mercedes, my children Joshua and Joseph and to my bonus kids Lawrence Jr. Kenny, Lexi and Lauren. I love you all and thank you for your support and believing in me

My maternal grandmother Blossie, along with my mother, was a female role model for me growing. She provided unconditional love, strength, endurance and always gave us little nuggets of wisdom. ***She was my first best friend/Girlfriend*** even though I had siblings and tons of cousins. She was special. Blossie was married off at the age of 12 to my widowed grandfather Doy who had two children already. She raised those two as her own and gave birth to fourteen children which she had from the age of thirteen to forty-one. Her faith in God was unwavering.

As early as I can remember from my spending time with my grandmother, she was the first to rise and the last one to go to sleep. At night she would walk through the house accounting for everyone and everything. She put herself last. Her joy was serving her family. She said it was her calling to make sure her family started their day with a meal that stuck to their guts. Her saying: "A good breakfast starts a good day," is something I live by and believe in. I could be in the kitchen with her for hours making meals and desserts. It was her way of cooking and baking up love. Blossie would say, "Everyone needs a good meal, kind words, and a little love," and she believed she could give a bit of all three during suppertime.

I stand on my mother's shoulders as she stood on Blossies. Grandma Blossie would say to me "The sacrifices I make during my lifetime will bless my family for many generations." I'd asked her how and she answered "I vowed as a young girl to love unconditionally. My children and grandchildren will always know and feel love." She then proceeded to tell me as a child that she never felt loved. She said it was because she was married off so very young. Her brother had left at an early age and she never saw him again. She was heartbroken by this and vowed never to say the word "goodbye." She said "If any of my children or grandchildren come to me about anything I will not judge but love them unconditionally, even when they have done wrong until it is made right. Connie *Love can melt the coldest heart and it can move a nation. Love is so very powerful.*"

Blossie's Kind of Discipline

Blossie never spanked any of her grandchildren, but there were times I wished she would have just spanked me. She would give these long talks that would make you feel two inches tall by the time she finished with you. I did not want to repeat the same mistakes with her again. Seeing the disappointment in her face was horrible. My grandmother could **read** you so very well that it wasn't until you walked away that you realized that she had given you a piece of her mind and put you in your place. All of this was done with soft spoken and kind words. She would tell you that she loved you and expected better out of you. You would have to promise not let whatever you did happen again. Then before she would let you go she would say "don't let me have to pray about you". Blossie was truly a praying woman and I did not *want her to ever pray about me!*

Chase Your Dreams Until They Come True
Blossie encouraged me to pursue my dreams at an early age. She said anything is possible so chase your dreams and make them come true. She was my cheerleader and my accomplishments were her accomplishments. Grandmama, as we would also refer to her, would reward us with the best deserts and put a few dollars in our pocket in a tied-up handkerchief for simple accomplishments. When I say she was my first cheerleader… this woman would have me all puffed up when I walked away from her believing I could do anything. I wanted to

become a cheerleader in middle school but it was expensive and I was afraid that if I made it I would be the only black girl on the squad. Her advice was: "So what, and what is stopping you? We as family, we will make it work and you be that proud black girl out there. One day it will be several black girls doing the same thing." Yes I made the team and was the only one for a few years even in high school.

Blossie was a faith talking and visionary woman. I still look back in awe of the things she said and her nuggets of wisdom. I still apply this experience to my life now when I face opportunities where I am the minority as a woman or African American.

I only saw my grandmother cry once at my Uncle Eugene's funeral. She said there was no pain like burying your child. Blossie had lost two children she birthed as a teenager before they were one year old. I remember asking her the day after Uncle Eugene's funeral if she was going to be alright. Her reply was

"Life goes on and there was family to take care for. I will mourn Gene in my quiet time." Her strength was unbelievable. For her the family needs came first. I often saw her put her feelings aside. Today we would say, "Put your game face on and confront the world as if nothing happened." I would see her many times on the front porch in deep thought and after Uncle Gene's death I knew not to bother her during her quiet time. This was her way of reenergizing for a new day.

Blossie's Advice on My First Love

Blossie witnessed my first real love. We will call him Jessie for this story. She told me Jessie was going to go places and would be very successful, but that I would not take that journey with him. Grandma said he would make me happy for now *with his charming self.* She also enjoyed his company and he would bring her treats. One day he bought her a house dress and house shoes which gave her the biggest smile. She chuckled the next day and said *we* are going to enjoy him while it last. At that moment I wondered if Jessie was dating me or my grandmother. I dated Jessie off and on for six years. I so wanted this relationship to work, but in the end Blossie was right it never worked out. Jessie is still a great guy and she was right. He is very successful and has a beautiful family.

I lost my first best friend/girlfriend on August 31, 1984. Blossie's nuggets of wisdom still play a big part in my life and have been passed on to my children and will soon be passed on to my grandchildren. I can still hear her voice saying "Connie, remember love is your most powerful weapon. You love your family with all that is within you and when you feel you can't love no more then God will increase your heart to love when it's not in you to do."

Special Thank you to my pre-sale supporters

Lawrence Peltier

Mercedes Jones

James Sturgis Sr.

Penelope Linley

Kenneth Peltier

Charlotte Walker

Sheila Reese

Veleta Bowen

Djuana Jefferson

Charles Jones

Lawrence Peltier Jr.

Joshua Perry

Joseph Perry

Ashely McClure

Wake Up Girlfriend

Jennifer Keeling-Miggins

Harold and Michelle Keeling

Connie McCain

Wanda Williams

Hewitt- McClure Family Chiropractor

Bridgett Pitts

Douglas and Trina Smith

Prentice and LaChelle Ackey

Vickie Dobbs

Tracy Danley Williams

Tracy and Edward Coleman

Angelo Turner

Kaime Slade

Chapter 7.

April Y. Cunningham

Two Questions and a Statement

To my Savior ~ for YOUR grace, mercy and the love of words! To MY Girlfriends ~ our journeys have made me a better woman.

A Girlfriends Outing or a Girls Night Out event has been planned and you are excited about going. You are at work thinking about your day and all the things that you must finish to make sure that you are ready for the evening. You pause for moment... Thinking about the two critical questions that every girlfriend must ask before she makes the decision to go. What do you think they are? Even if not said aloud...you thought it. I know I do! And depending on the answers it determines whether you decide to go.

In my experience those two questions are as follows:

    1. Who's going?
    2. What are you wearing?

Did I get those right? Depending upon the names that are provided to question number one, this key statement immediately follows... "I'm riding shot gun!!" Is that true? Have you done it? Be honest.

Presentation is key and looking FINER, as defined by my sorority, is a must. For those that know me, have seen my office, my car or my social media pages there are two pieces of my wardrobe that are must haves. Shoes and hats. Either together for the #CoordinationFactor or as a stand-alone for #Shoegame or #Hattitude wow factors.

My love for shoes was simply born from the fact that growing up I did not have many pairs of shoes. I made a promise to myself at young age that once I was grown and could afford them, that I would get as many as I wanted and in whatever color that I wanted. Thus, "A ShoeDiva" 👠 was born. I dreamed about it and I definitely delivered on my promise!!

Now these Hats...are a whole different story. It's not only the type of hat that you wear, it's the color, the 45 degree "tilt" that you wear it and the confidence and poise that you must possess to pull off the hat. Not everyone can, but those that do make a statement.

My journey in learning about hats has been such an important and powerful part of my life. It has caused me to look through a different lens about images and relationships both literally and figuratively.

It is the figurative part that has inspired me to tell my story and how it relates to the many hats we wear and the roles that we play in those girlfriend relationships.

My first introduction to hats was as young girl growing up in the church. My Godmother, the First Lady of the church, "Mrs. F". (may she rest in peace), wore one faithfully every Sunday. I noticed that she had them on, but I never paid much attention to them. Fast-forward a few years to my teens and my other Godmother, "Mrs. L." (may she also rest in peace) taught me about Jesus which saved my life. She and many of the other church mothers taught me about hats. They wore big beautiful hats, colored with sparkles and bows....... ones that I vowed that I would never be caught in, except for in my casket! Well, how many of you know that you should never say never, as it may just come back around and be your thing. Just like me wearing hats today. Ohhh, how we mature and live. Our life experiences and lessons give us a different perspective. As we grow, our taste, our vision, our inspiration changes and so has my love for hats.

It's now the year 2006. I've made it! I'm a successful HR executive, a blessed wife to the most awesome man in the world, a mother to my two gifts from God, #TeamCunninghamROCKS. And I have more shoes than you can count! What more could a girl ask for....Girlfriends, of course!!!!!

"How many of us have them? Ones you can depend on." – Whodini

I have many Girlfriends. I am fortunate to be surrounded by some powerful, beautiful, and influential Girlfriends who have supported me and embraced me like I was family and I have returned that blessing of supporting them as well. My two of the 3 Musketeers of which I am Number three (because I am the youngest). My Seventh-Day Adventist Church Girlfriends. My Slippery Rock University Girlfriends. My Girlfriends that I have made in each of the cities that I lived in (PA, MN & NC). My Human Resources Girlfriends and my "Oh Sooo Sweet" sorors of Zeta Phi Beta Sorority, Incorporated. I think that covers all my Girlfriends.

Now back to the Girlfriends Night Out.

We bought tickets to a small stage play at the Actor's Theater of Charlotte entitled "Crowns." The play followed the lives of six Southern African-American women (Girlfriends). The play focused on hat etiquette, style, and attitude but it also shed light on the relationships that women have, the issues that they face and the triumphs/testimonies that come out of our journeys.

One year later, I was nostalgic when I was cast in a local version "Crowns" for our church's Youth Federation in Durham, NC. I had the honor of playing the role of "Jeanette" a sassy character with style and wit. My two Girlfriends and I signed up for the play. Jeannette, Yolanda and Mabel, traveled up and down I-85 from Charlotte to Raleigh for four long months, getting crash courses in acting 101, singing 101 and stage cues 101 to begin preparing for the stage play.

The experience of participating in the play was a calculated risk for me. I was stepping out of my comfort zone to do something that I have never done before. I was comfortable speaking in front of groups at work, church, in the community and occasionally in an afternoon skit at church. This play was on a totally different level and it ultimately caused me to evaluate the hats that I wear and the roles & responsibilities that come with them. I learned so much about myself and the intricacies of women. The phases and emotions that we go through in happy, sad and even in stressful times. The most important lesson that I took away from the preparation and culmination of the play was that when women (Girlfriends) put their collective minds together, we have the ability to birth a beautiful masterpiece that gets brought forth and delivered flawlessly.

The hats in the play symbolized the joys, the struggles, the pride and the strength that enabled them to survive and preserve their dignity. The same lesson can be applied when we take inventory of the Girlfriends we have in our lives. The ones who have been there since the playground. The ones who become your blood sister by poking your finger with the safety pin and touching pinkies. The ones who wiped your tears after your first heartbreak. Those ones who you walk across the graduation stage with. The maids of honor and Godmothers to your children. The Girlfriend list goes on and on. It is not about who you've known the longest, but who has been there and who is still there. We have all lost some along the way and it is okay.

> *Everything comes into your life for a reason, a season or a lifetime. You must understand and accept that everyone can't go on the journey with you. – unknown*

There is a time for everything, and a season for every activity under the heavens:
2. a time to be born and a time to die,
a time to plant and a time to uproot,
3. a time to kill and a time to heal,
a time to tear down and a time to build,
4. a time to weep and a time to laugh,
a time to mourn and a time to dance,
5. a time to scatter stones and a time to gather them, a time to embrace and a time to refrain from embracing,
6. a time to search and a time to give up,
a time to keep and a time to throw away,
7. a time to tear and a time to mend,
a time to be silent and a time to speak,
8. a time to love and a time to hate,
a time for war and a time for peace.

– Ecclesiastes 3:1-8

Think about your family, your friends your Sister Friends, Your BFF's, your Ride or Dies. The ones in the front row, those in the balcony, those you only go out with when there are two to three other people going. Whatever you call them they play an integral part in your life. Right???

When I think about my Girlfriends, I get excited about the relationships, the joys, laughs, the love and even the tears because they become our testimonies. How many of you remember this song? *"Thank you for being a Friend, we traveled down the road and back again. Your heart is true, you're a pal and confidant. And if we threw a party and invited everyone you knew you would see the biggest gift would be from me and the card attached would say... Thank you for being a Friend"* Thank you Golden Girls!

Now it is time to take inventory. Take a look at the relationships that you have right now in your life. Count how much time, energy and money that you dedicate to each of them. What roles have you played? Have you been the doctor, the lawyer, the therapist, the coach, the encourager, the motivator, given the tough love or just been that listening ear? Whew, that's a lot of work. How many hats are you wearing right now?

Even though we feel that we must be our sister's keeper it is important that we make ourselves a priority. It is in us to put everyone first and we sometimes get the short end of the stick. It is this compassion that makes us women and Girlfriends. However, we have to make time for ourselves and understand that we matter too. Visualize this scene. You get on the plane for a trip and the door closes. The flight attendant comes over the intercom and says these words, "In the event that plane loses cabin pressure the oxygen masks will fall from the ceiling. Place the mask over your nose and mouth pull the band over your head and pull the straps tight. Make sure your put your mask on before helping someone else." The airlines are onto something and we have to follow that same guidance. If we don't take care of ourselves we won't be good to anyone.

So, the question becomes do you really need Girlfriends? This exercise may help you answer that question. This is the place that you get to have active participation in the book. You'll need your hand for this.

Exercise: Cover your left ear with your left hand and read each of these statements aloud to yourself and then repeat them in your head, as if you were repeating after me:

- *Having girlfriends and being a part of a sisterhood is hard work.*
- *My girlfriends are weaved in the many stories of my life.*
- *We wear many hats in each relationships and sometimes it is too much.*

- *When I need to, they allow me to really be me – good, bad or indifferent.*
- *Sometimes they keep secrets and ask too many questions... in my business.*
- *They will drive through blizzards, rain, sleet, snow and the dark of night to get me when my hour of need.*
- *They don't always tell me that I am right BUT they are usually honest.*
- *They sometimes push, pull, lift, pull down, pray and yell, cheer and intervene.*

Ok, you can uncover your ear. I just want to make sure it was clear and didn't go in one ear and out the other. ☺ So, after all those statements that we say (sometimes only to ourselves) do you need girlfriends or not? I know that I do, and many other girlfriends agree.

It is up to you – <u>Insert your name here</u> to make the decision on how you will make a difference in your girlfriend relationships

"Research shows that women, [possibly] more than men, need to maintain those connections. It increases serotonin and oxytocin, the bonding hormone," says Alisa Ruby Bash, PsyD, LMFT. "Maintaining those bonds becomes even more important as we grow older," according to Dr. Bash. "We get busier, with more responsibilities," she says. "It makes us feel nurtured and validated to hang out with friends we can be totally ourselves [with], minus the outside pressures."

We need girlfriends because:

- They laugh at the same silly things we do.
- They can be petty with us even if it is only for 2 minutes.
- They give honest advice even it hurts.

- They will be there for us even if we are in different states and miles apart.
- They will get Vaseline and rubber bands (to protect our hair and face) IF we need to fight.

AND

- They will celebrate with us when we are winning and at our best but will still love us when we are at our worst.

Maya Angelou said it best in the poem *Alone*. "Alone, all alone. Nobody, but nobody can make it out here alone." That is precisely why we need our Girlfriends. Every Girlfriend has one and every Girlfriend needs one, if not more.

So, on this girlfriend journey, we've navigated through shoes, hats, children, and spouses but I'll end where we started.... What will be your two questions and your statement that you ask and make about your Girlfriends?

"My Friends have made the story of my life. In a thousand ways they have turned my limitations into beautiful privileges." – Helen Keller

Special Thank you to my pre-sale supporters

Janelle Elam

Jennifer Alexander

Soror Tracey Headen

Soror Deadra Brown Cherry

Andrea Martin ~ Discovering my Wings, LLC

Ursula Pizarro

Ulysesa Sweatt

Carmella Crews

Anita Collins

Ashley D.

Michael T. Howze

Keisha Unger

Soror Aritha Richardson

TeamCunningham

Tracey Rhoney

Renee Clayton Jones

Jazmine Borden

Will Bray

Dr. BT

Rob Harding

Christina Forbes

Kim Carlisle

Heather Johnson

Aurelia Addison

Shea Halstead

Cheryl Davis

Wanda Villenuava

Greg Weatherbee

Diana Rhine

Pastor & Sis Mitchell

Lynn Pinder

Lynn Gilmer

Stefanie Austin

Ashleigh Conteh

Althea Battle

H Terrence Bardouille

Soror Shellisa Multrie

Soror Kimberlee Archie

Cindy Mendez

Sarah Taylor

Muriel Desiree

Patrick Carter

Shona Robinson

Dorian Barnes

Venus Jackson

Trina Henderson

Alice Barber

Jamillah Ford

Serena Dean

Alice Smith

Denise Jones

Ophelia Henry

Wake Up Girlfriend

Chapter 8.

Yvonne Smith

Growth in Friendship

Dedicated to my sister-friends that helped to grow and shape my idea of friendship!
Thank you!

When I was first approached with the idea of being a contributing author to this book, I immediately thought to myself, "I'll pass! Thanks, but, no thanks." Not because I'm not a fun loving, spirited, vivacious woman with loads of personality (seriously) and a lot to say but, because I'm 45 years old and I don't have many friends, let alone girlfriends. I lamented over this project and what I would share because I had this image of what girlfriend-ship looked like and my relationships don't fit that mold. For me, I think of girlfriends as a group of women that get together on a regular basis and share their successes, failures, ups, downs, accomplishments, etc… They dish the tea/gossip (yes, gossip), eat together, drink together, shop together, cry together, laugh heartily and love mightily like on the old 'Girlfriends' television show or the movie 'Waiting to Exhale'. They are cherished relationships, the kind that warm your heart as you reminisce. The kind I've witnessed from afar with envy, albeit in person or via social media on Facebook or Instagram. As I thought long and hard about what to share, the painful reality set in that perhaps I lack the qualifications to participate in this project because again, I don't have an 'oooh....ahh' experience to share that will fully engage the reader. You see, I don't know what it's like to accompany a group of friends on a real 'Girls Trip' and I don't have any one or two girlfriends that I sit and talk with on the phone, over lunch/dinner or each other's homes on a regular basis. As I continued to think about what to share, I had an epiphany and told myself, "You don't have girlfriends because you're insecure and refuse to give of your WHOLE self." YIKES! That stung but, I'm sure someone reading this right now either sees themselves in my revelation or they're wondering...what does she mean?

Allow me to explain….

I am my mother's only child so growing up in my home there was always me, myself and I. That is until my childhood friends came over, spend the night/weeks and then went home. I was by all accounts an 'only child' and it was often a lonely existence. My immediate family was small in numbers and I wasn't raised in a family where there was lots of activity and people sharing stories, laughs, tears, etc. I learned early on how to rely on myself for my emotional needs. I learned how to express myself and my inner most thoughts by scribing because that way I wouldn't have to explain my feelings or get permission to feel the way that I did. I'd write poetry and keep it in a folder, never to be discussed. Those were my feelings, my thoughts, my dreams, because I chose to write my emotions, as you can imagine I was very good at not non-verbal expression as a child/teenager. Trust me, my non-verbal communication could tell the WHOLE story (laughing). Unfortunately, these same traits and limitations grew with me into adulthood.

As far as my friends were concerned, growing up I was that one friend that all my friends could count on for the honest truth. They would often tell other people, "If you don't want to hear the truth don't ask Vonnie" and that was the truth. I was the one that would give it to them straight with no chaser. My opinion mattered and was provided whether solicited or not. Looking back, chile I was THAT friend. I was the girlfriend that would do prank three-way phone calls to bust the boyfriends in lies. I was the friend that was ready to fight for MY friends. I was always the smallest in the bunch but, I would ride or die for my childhood friends. I would not let anyone bully MY friends. I stood up for them and would be the voice for them. When I was bullied for a little while by a boy that liked me, I put rocks in my metal

Strawberry Shortcake lunchbox and beat the tar out of him for bullying me. When it worked, I told my best friend in elementary school to do the same thing to the people that bullied her too. As a teenager, I listened as they'd share their heartbreaks and darkest most painful experiences in their homes. I'd cry with them and plot revenge for them (so glad I've grown). I was a leader but, what most of my childhood friends don't know to this day is that as an adult I can say I've learned so much more from them than they ever have from me.

I'm sure most of us can agree that much of who we are as children and teenagers carries into our adult lives. Why? Because those experiences are all we've come to know. They mold our thinking and shape our reality. They define us into adulthood until life and maturity sweeps through like a thief in the night to rob us of our youth. For me, this was true. Into adulthood I carried that same level of privacy. I struggled with verbally expressing my inner most thoughts and challenges. It wasn't important for me to share what I was going through – only what my friends were experiencing. I was good at that! I was good at listening. I was good at offering advice. Like many, I shared what I wanted to share but never at the expense of ***fully exposing my deepest, darkest vulnerabilities***. I would always say, "I just don't have the same need as my friends." I flourished at being the friend to help but, not necessarily allow others to help me and until not long ago I was truly ok with that. I basked in that role. That is until a few years ago, when a childhood sister-friend of 30 plus years and I had a major blow up/blow out and I will never forget her words as she said, "You are so selfish!" Because our personalities are both very strong there were MANY other words exchanged but, that statement hit me the hardest. At the time, I was thinking she was crazy as hell. What did she mean – selfish? In my mind I was one of the best damn friends she ever had. I was always there for her. I listened and showed up when she needed me as a child, teenager and adult but, the reality is I didn't, and I know that now.

Years passed and this friend and I went without speaking. We went without communication of any kind for that matter and I was ok with that. I was ok with no communication because I wasn't a communicator so hell, it worked for me. I would ignore her posts on social media and allow my petty to come into play at times. When people would ask me how she was doing I would simply say, "I don't know! We haven't spoken in a while. Perhaps you should ask her." Most that know us both were often surprised by my response because we were *forever friends*.

Fast forward several years later, I finally understood what she meant by selfish. This revelation did not come while driving home or through a favorite song or via an 'ah ha' (snaps fingers) moment. It came after experiencing a one-sided friendship with another person. It came after I had allowed myself to be vulnerable with someone and they 'shaded' me. It came after I had truly been there for someone and wasn't appreciated or thanked for just being a friend. It came after I sacrificed so much for someone I hadn't known nearly as long, encouraged them through their rough times and dark days and they were nowhere to be found when I needed them. It came when my husband told me I needed to move on from that relationship because she wasn't a friend and was incapable of being one. It came when I realized there was no reciprocity. The signs had been written on the wall for several years that she and I were just acquaintances but, I ignored the signs because I desperately wanted to be a better friend. The relationship she and I shared was going to be the relationship where I proved to myself that I knew how to be a friend. As the adage goes *'hindsight is always 20/20.'* Truth is, **she wasn't a good friend to me**. I deserved better because I gave more the same way my childhood friend(s) did. Our relationships shared a common theme: one-sidedness and that cut like a knife.

> *"The weak can never forgive. Forgiveness is the attribute of the strong."* – *Mahatma Gandhi*

Several years ago, I contacted a different childhood sister-friend and asked for her forgiveness in regard to how I treated her and our friendship at a time when I was at my lowest. Instead of sharing what I was going through since my diagnosis of Multiple Sclerosis, I shut down. I became angry and shunned away those that simply wanted to help. She forgave me and we are now in much better place. For that, I am grateful! Then, almost two years ago the friend I referred to earlier and I had an opportunity to talk. We cried (snot nosed cried) and I owned up to my actions. I apologized from the depths of my soul for how I treated our sisterhood and she too has forgiven me. I am so appreciative, not just for their forgiveness, but, for the overall experiences and the opportunity to make right my mistreatment of them. I am and will forever be grateful for their love for me, their example of strength and their ability to accept/forgive me.

As I said earlier, I've learned so much from my childhood friends. From them, I have grown tremendously as a woman and as a friend. I decided to share this experience with you in hopes that it challenges you think about your friendships and your contributions to them. Honor the women in your lives and your friendships/sisterhoods. Don't be a one-sided friend. ***Take risks! Expose yourself. Open your mouth, talk, share and allow them to be***

a friend to you. Know this, if you remain closed to the idea of sharing every part of you, you will forever be lonely. Your true friends want to see you happy and they want to share in your WHOLE being! As you reflect on your relationships be honest about the treatment of those you claim to love. If you've not been a fair friend be accountable. Offer a genuine apology but, remember **"...*Sacrifice is at the heart of repentance. Without deeds your apology is worthless...*"** so once you've apologized commit to the process of friendship. If someone has dishonored you in friendship forgive them. I am still a work in progress but, there is freedom in forgiveness and I *know* there is healing in transparency.

There is nothing on this earth more to be prized than true friendship" – Thomas Aquinas

Wake up Girlfriend… Your friends need ALL OF YOU!

Special Thank you to my pre-sale supporters

Akeylee Smith

Dyani Richberg

Tonia Holloway

Lisa Madden

Pamela Washington

Carlie Cross

Dyanna Craighead

Sabrina Schuler

Yasmeen Cooper

Zakia Shareef

Kalandra Thompson

Wake Up Girlfriend

Conclusion

The League of Girlfriends organization which I founded on September 16, 2016 has in many ways restored my faith in friendships. As I mentioned earlier I've always had really good female and male friendship. All of which were long standing. I was never the type to meet someone right off and feel comfortable enough to call them a friend. Again, I believed that you "Can't get no new old Friends!"

Through the process of creating this collaboration project God once again showed me the power of connecting soles. This "Girlfriend" thing really works and it is awesome. By the third week of this collaboration project these girlfriends were discussing taking a trip together and on one Saturday morning I woke up late to find numerous messages on my phone from our group chat. These messages were of encouragement, love and support for one girlfriend who was struggling that morning with depression. This is more evidence that **Every woman needs and deserves good girlfriends**.

I can do all things through Christ who strengthens me ~ Phil 4:13

Thank you

I am most grateful to my Lord and Savior Jesus Christ who has brought me this far in spite of myself. Everything I do, everything I have and everything I am is because of you.

To my seasoned Girlfriends: my mother, the late Carena M. Phillips, my Nana the late Honorable Evelyn D. Ricardson, my great grandmother Carena King, my grandmothers the late Francis Anderson and Margaret Anderson. My beautiful mother Toni Anderson and her sisters Aunt Vernie, Aunt Rona, Aunt Beverly and Aunt Tara. My mother-in-law Sharon Montgomery, Godmother Azalia, Mrs. P and Jasmine. Along with my numerous pretend Aunts: Rose, Trudie, Tina, Kathy, Phillapa, Micki and my big sister Lynn, Oshoon and many more. It was watching your interactions that showed me the many sides of girlfriends. The way you could fight like dogs and love each other in the same breath. Borrow a cup of sugar or feed each other's kids for days on end without conflict. All in love. I use you as my examples daily.

To the men that stayed out of the way. My husband Dion, my pop the late T.R. Richardson and my mentor and friend my daddy, Tony Anderson. My ace - my father-in-law Manford Sims. Also Uncle Mike, Uncle Al, Uncle Jimmy, Uncle Wayne, Uncle Miller and the late Uncle Smitty.

To my siblings Mann, Geron, Nathan, Leslie, Aja, and Ish. I love you all and pray that you each get the desires of you hearts. To my best friends forever Trish, Tawnya, Ruthie and Donnet. To my perfect children, grandbabies, nieces, nephews, Goddaughters; Ericka, Lataja, Ashley, Nelly, Nate, Brianna, Jasmine, Bub, Keion, Talor, London, Christian aka Smooch, Tristen, Kam, Aspyn, JoJo, Jaeda and Kyrie.

About the Creator

Author, Professional Speaker, Founder of the League of Girlfriends, Achievement Coach and Master Planner.

Angie is a two time author who had been transforming the lives of women for over 20 years. She most recently founded the League of Girlfriends social organization for the everyday woman who has moved to the ATL tristate and left their girlfriends back home. She realized that women need to be connected socially. Founded in September 2016 the League of Girlfriends has eight locations around the country and has been visited by thousands of women with the desire to find local girlfriends to share DYI workshops, local outings and retreats.

Over 20 years ago Angie founded *Angela's Exquisite Events*, the premier wedding/event planner company. During this time she spent over 14 years a business leader at Morgan Stanley and its predecessor firms where she transformed mindsets of executes and employees in her various roles.

She has also been a transformational achievement coach for all of her adult life using her special gift of assisting people to discover what they were brought here to do, empower them into execution.

Angie moved to Atlanta over four years ago after she and her husband served together in founding a very successful pop warner Junior Football program in Northern New Jersey and as Chairs of Community Baptist Church of Englewood's Married Couples ministry where Angie also served as Chair of the Events Ministry for the church's 5,000+ membership.

In addition to her many functions as founder of the fastest growing women's organization in Atlanta, the League of Girlfriends she is the Executive Board Vice President of the oldest women's networking organization in Georgia, the Atlanta Women's Network.

She and her husband Dion of 12 years live in Acworth, GA with their 10 year old son Christian aka Smooch.

More on Angie CJ Sims

Angie Sims is available to be hired as a professional speaker, your achievement coach, or an event planner. If interested please email her at LeagueofGirlfriends@gmail.com

Angie speaks on the following topics:

- Mastering Relationships for Success
- Leading them Through the Fire
- Live your Purpose NOW – Discovery to K.I.M.
- Wake UP Girlfriend, you're missing you!
- Keeping God in your success

Follow Angie on Social Media

Facebook.com & LinkedIn.com - Angela Sims
Instagram.com, Twitter.com - @FindGirlfriends

Visit her websites:

www.leagueofgirlfriends.com

Made in the USA
Columbia, SC
23 April 2019